GEORGE SZIRTES
In the Land of the Giants

GEORGE SZIRTES was born in Budapest in 1948 and came to England with his refugee family in 1956 following the Hungarian Uprising. He was brought up in London and studied fine art in various art schools. His first book for adults, *The Slant Door*, appeared in 1979 and was joint-winner of the Faber Memorial Prize. He has published some thirteen books of poems since including *Reel*, which was awarded the T.S. Eliot Prize for 2004, *New and Collected Poems* (2008) and *The Burning Books* (2009) that was shortlisted for the Eliot Prize. He has translated all kinds of books from the Hungarian and edited some anthologies too. His book of poems for children *The Red All Over Riddle Book* was published in 1997. He lives in Norfolk.

Also by George Szirtes

POETRY FOR ADULTS
An English Apocalypse
Reel
New and Collected poems
The Burning of the Books and Other Poems
Shuck, Hick, Tiffey

POETRY FOR CHILDREN
The Red All Over Riddle Book

GEORGE SZIRTES

In the Land of the Giants

SELECTED CHILDREN'S POEMS

Illustrated by Helen Szirtes

SALT

CROMER

PUBLISHED BY SALT PUBLISHING
12 Norwich Road, Cromer, Norfolk NR27 0AX
United Kingdom

All rights reserved

© George Szirtes, 2012
Illustrations © Helen Szirtes

The right of George Szirtes to be identified as the
editor of this work has been asserted by him in accordance
with Section 77 of the Copyright, Designs and Patents Act 1988.

This book is in copyright. Subject to statutory exception
and to provisions of relevant collective licensing
agreements, no reproduction of any part may take
place without the written permission of Salt Publishing.

First published 2012

Printed in Great Britain by Clays Ltd, St Ives plc

Typeset in Oneleigh 11 / 14

*This book is sold subject to the conditions that it shall not,
by way of trade or otherwise, be lent, re-sold, hired out,
or otherwise circulated without the publisher's prior consent
in any form of binding or cover other than that in which
it is published and without a similar condition including this
condition being imposed on the subsequent purchaser.*

ISBN 978 1 84471 451 3 paperback

1 3 5 7 9 8 6 4 2

Tom, Helen, Marlie and Lukas

CONTENTS

Acknowledgements   xi

Four Superstitions   1
  1. The Sneezing Week   1
  2. Watch who you are winking at   2
  3. Bad signs   3
  4. Runs till it drops   4
Three Fires and a Flood   6
  Flame   6
  The Great Fire of London   7
  The Fire's Heart   9
  The Flood   10
The Bee's Knees   12
  The Bee's Knees   12
  The Wasp's Waist   13
  The Serpent's Tail   14
  The Fish's Fingers   15
  The Bicycle's Wrists   16
  The Clouds' Hair   17
  The Wind's Face   18
  The Sea's Hands   19
  The Sun's Toes   20
  The Cold's Teeth   21
  The Refrigerator's Belly   22
  The Wall's Ears   23
  The Bedroom Chest   24

The Clothes-hanger's Collarbone	25
The Book's Spine	26
The Window's Eyes	28
The Butcher's Calves	29
The Bottle's Neck	30
The Cup's Lip	31
The Ice Cream's Tongue	32
The Cave's Mouth	33
The Lake's Bottom	34
Three Mysteries	35
1. The Lost Sock Mystery	35
2. The Mystery of the Ant	36
3. The Rainbow Mystery	37
In the Land of the Giants	38
Rock A Bye	38
Beware Of The Bear!	39
In The Land Of Giants	40
At Gran's	41
Fancy Dress	42
Henry	43
Brave	44
Pianist	45
Soulful	46
Flautist	47
Plumbing Service	48
Egg Magic	49

The Great Drongo	50
Poet	51
No, Love	52
Visitor	53
Miss String	55
Ahem	56
Old Couples	58
Whoopsa	60
Moonlife	61
Moon Questions	61
Space Comes Out at Night	63
Apple Tree	65
Mouse Dreaming	66
Goldfish	67
Animal Lore	68
The Wreck of The Hope	69
From the Hungarian	70
Bird	70
The Spring	71
The Earth	72
Ant	73
A Poem about Two Seals	74
Winter Trees	75
Storks	76
Snail	77
The Bear's Dilemma	79

Three Short Verses About the Wind	80
Sleighbells	81
Deep in the Wood the Violets Drowse	82
My Dog Ace	83
Happy New Year	84

ACKNOWLEDGEMENTS

Some of these poems first appeared in *The Red-All-Over Riddle Book*. The poems from Hungarian first appeared in *Sheep Don't Go To School* edited by Andrew Fusek Peters.

In the Land of Giants

FOUR SUPERSTITIONS

1. THE SNEEZING WEEK

He who sneezes twice on Monday
Finds a lost sock in his shoe.

Sneezing even once on Tuesday
Both your ears fill up with glue.

Wednesday sneezing can be lucky
Providing that it isn't flu.

Those who sneeze three times on Thursday
See their fondest dreams come true.

Friday sneezing means a meeting:
A sneezer geezer meeting you.

Saturday's not good for sneezing.

Sunday sneezing just won't do.

2. WATCH WHO YOU ARE WINKING AT

>Wink at a dog
>Fall in a bog.
>
>Wink at a cat
>Lose your hat.
>
>Wink at a slug
>Slip on the rug.
>
>Wink at a fish
>Get your wish
>
>Wink at a rabbit
>Develop a habit.

In the Land of Giants

3. BAD SIGNS

When the wind runs through the garden, when the ants troop
 down the street
When the spider in the window has eight legs but just six feet
When the sheep all start to bark and every dog begins to bleat
Count your toes, open your eyes,
Check your pulse, put out your spies,
Watch where you're going.

When the chickens pack their jimjams, when the pig stands up
 to beg
When the butcher sells you chocolate and the baker lays an egg
When the table starts complaining and demands an extra leg
Cross your fingers, mop the floor
Wash your hands and slam the door,
Better get going.

When elephants throughout all China suddenly turn black
 and white
When the car locked in the garage goes out by itself at night
When the mouse on the savannah gives the lion a nasty bite
Pack your bags, empty your pockets,
Light the candle, set off the rockets
On your marks. Set. Get going.

4. RUNS TILL IT DROPS

It never rains but when it's wet.
Slow drying glue is rarely *fast*.
A flower is up when it's in *bed*.
A gift's a present though it's *past*.

A beaten fish knows when it's *battered*.
An ice cream knows when it is *licked*.
A tired window can look *shattered*.
A clock's in order when it's *ticked*.

The wrong road is the one you've *crossed*.
A proper map is a *relief*.
You rule the roost when you're em*bossed*.
Hankies obey their handker*chief*.

Leopards may hide but will be *spotted*.
The tiger always earns its *stripes*.
Meat on cue is often *potted*.
Wind whistles but water *pipes*.

Dad's bald patch is top of the *pops*.
A hairy lamb grows *muttonchops*.
A wood's arrested by the *copse*.
The stopper leaks until it *stops*.

Your nose runs for you till it drops!!!

GEORGE SZIRTES

THREE FIRES AND A FLOOD

FLAME

Fire
Multiplies
Fire makes fire
A whole leaping choir
Fire wider and higher
Watching the sparks fly
Watching smoke rise
Each hiss and flicker
A spreadable snicker
But there, there
Without air
Fire dies
No spark
Just dark
Wick
Stick
Thick
Dark

Gone

THE GREAT FIRE OF LONDON

Thomas Farynor, Baker to the King,
Left his oven burning with the firewood nearby.
The embers muttered, the little flames took wing
And sang to the bigger flames, Come with us and fly!

So fly they did, from the Baker to The Star,
To The Star next door in Fish Street, in one almighty flap,
From there on to St Margaret's which wasn't very far,
The little flames kept hopping from gap to narrow gap.

Here lay the tallow, the spirits and the straw,
Here lay the coal and the hemp and the oil,
Given a decent breeze the fire began to draw,
And soon barrels full of water were coming to the boil.

How happy were the flames, the gleeful little pests,
They sang and crowed and whistled in full throat,
Flashing now their wings and now their bright red breasts,
Like robins who had never sung a note.

By now their bigger cousins were roosting on the bridge,
Old London Bridge was burning and the Thames was
    molten lead,
But the firebirds kept leaping the gap from ridge to ridge,
Till the city blazed from roof to riverbed.

Oh it was spectacular, those flames up to their tricks,
And the mess they left behind them was desolate and vague.
For days they screeched and bellowed in 1666,
And wiped away whole districts, but also purged the Plague,

Or so they told each other when the squawking had died down,
And whether it was accident or fate
They certainly had changed the face of the whole town
Before they settled back into the grate.

THE FIRE'S HEART

You think you can sometimes see it
for a moment at the tip of red
where you think it's hottest,

and it is clearly beating, steady as a drum,
echoing your own heart which, by extension,
is pure flame.

If only you could touch it, put your finger to it
but it is forbidden, dangerous,
and wholly momentary,

perhaps even illusion. And yet
something goes on beating and is hot,
and fire exists as must the heart,
must it not?

THE FLOOD

And then it did fall
    Yes it did fall
        At first fitful
            Then a fistful
Fell like crystal
    Broken, brittle
        A faint rattle
            Glass and metal
Watch it mottle
    Watch it settle
        Mutter
            Spatter
To the letter
    Ever wetter
        Wider water
            Filling each and every quarter

Well above the usual quota
    From Peru to
        Minnesota
            And Dakota
As if by rota
    Enough to bloat a
    Whale or float a
            Fleet or a flotilla

In the Land of Giants

Sail and oar and deck and tiller
    Like some universal filler
        Without a filter
            Leaving the dry world out of kilter.

THE BEE'S KNEES

THE BEE'S KNEES

Great hairy knees bees have as they squat
in the flowers then push off with a spring,
all six knees pumping and shoving.
With so much power they're soon airborne, resilient,
muscular, adrift.

The bee's knees.

Brilliant.

THE WASP'S WAIST

The wasp's waist was so very thin
they thought they'd call the doctor in.

Kindly raise that stripy vest,
the doctor said, and tapped his chest
looked down his throat and prodded him.
I do agree you're far too slim.

You're thin just where you should be thick,
and although you're very sick
here's a pill should do the trick
which you should first grind down to paste
else you won't get it past that waist.
Take three a day. Now I must buzz.

But wasp did nothing of the kind.

No wasp does.

THE SERPENT'S TAIL

Being so very unlike a man
It's hard to know where I began
or where my body stopped,

Some time ago my head appeared
my eyes grew narrow, my lips sneered
the rest of me just flopped.

I wriggle, belly on the ground
I straighten out, I curl around,
Now I, now S, now O

Try as they can they always fail
To tell my body from my tail.
They try and try to no avail.
But will I tell them?
No.

THE FISH'S FINGERS

There was a time when fish had fingers
miniscule digits at the end of their fins,
which were useful to them for prising things open
for picking up coins and old rusted pins
for loosening fishermen's lines,
for pointing out notices and undersea signs . . .

and as for all the other uses the fishy nation
had for their fingers, I leave that to your imagination.

But some time back in the ice age,
which came as a terrible shock,
the sea turned into one vast frozen block
and their fingers dropped off to be trapped there
for thousands of years, maybe more,
lying in clumps on the cold ocean floor,

waiting to be harvested in our own time
by the few divers able
to descend to such depths and bring them
as delicacies to your table.

THE BICYCLE'S WRISTS

You must grip them carefully,
both at the same time
as though you were leading
a partner onto the dance floor

long slender arms extended
into the blue air of the street,
with just a touch of stiffness
as though neither of you
were sure of the steps.

So you wobble then move
on an impulse forwards
you and the wrists
hanging on for dear life

as if dancing were all
that kept you from falling.

THE CLOUDS' HAIR

Which can be brushed out long and fine
to lie across a pillow
or bunched and scrunched into an angry
knot of rain before it is undone,
when long hanks of it hang
over the horizon like curtains,
the whole sky shaking
its beautiful dense head.

THE WIND'S FACE

Suddenly appears before you round a corner
of the street, on a weekday, just as you are running
to school. Its mouth is wide, shouting something
you can't hear, its eyes screwed up,
wholly out of breath, cheeks red with the effort.

And it's bigger and fatter and flatter than you think,
and so fast you have hardly seen it but it's past you
or in you or at you like a paper bag blown
against you so tight its face might be your own.

THE SEA'S HANDS

The sea lays big glass hands on the sand,
spreading its fingers out as if new
to the shore. It can't quite believe in it.
It wants to hold on before the glass breaks.

And it does break, giggling with froth,
lets go and slips back as it always knew
it would and the waves clap their hands
erupting broad cream flakes

of pleasure into the air which is moving
and will move for ever, through
any fingers. And the sea doesn't mind.
It is the glass not the heart that breaks.

THE SUN'S TOES

The sun has dipped his toes into the sea.
It is far too cold for him
so he draws them out, and for a moment grows dim
and distant behind clouds. How far is he
from the fish under the waves, the rocks and wrecks
on the ocean floor?
He must find out and so he clears his decks
and steps in once more.

THE COLD'S TEETH

A biting cold, they say, and those clear
crisp little molars gnawing
at your ears and temples
or suddenly, in a cold snap,
furiously hacking
at your nose and finger ends.

Can you imagine them in the sky
in the eaves, in the earth itself
grinding away, milling down small,
tiny shark's teeth, dragon's teeth,
small pearls of ice

small miracles
glistening unwanted presents?

THE REFRIGERATOR'S BELLY

Always something going on in there,
little gurglings and slurps, and we feed it
all we have: butter, eggs, cheese, cold meats,
desserts in packets, tomatoes, spring onions,
left-overs, salads, ice-cubes, milkbottles.

What an investment. Its cold mouth shuts.
There's no throat, no gullet, all goes straight down
into the ice bucket of the belly, like Jonah or Gepetto,
the slow digestion working with sighs of resignation
and the waiting, waiting, waiting,

all that frozen wisdom, the opening of the door,
the world having ticked on with its comings and goings
and constant decaying.
Put your ear to the door. You can hear the meat
    thinking.
You can hear the cheese muttering.

Life inside the belly. Life inside the whale.

THE WALL'S EARS

Sometimes in a particular pattern or a patch of
    damp
You seem to see them, lit by the ceiling lamp.

Flat, subtle, sunken, all they have taken in
Swallowed with a muffled din,

Noises and voices settling between bricks.
Whatever has once sounded enters, sticks.

Like shells on the shore they echo but below
Your hearing thresh-hold so you never know

What tickled them, whatever pleased or hurt.
Their ears may listen but won't dish the dirt.

Whisper it now, watch them lean to hear,
and feel their patience, putting ear to ear.

THE BEDROOM CHEST

Think of its lungs puffed up with pillows,
breathing eiderdowns
settling like sachets.

The light flies in, the darkness flies out,
togs and feathers in endless conversation,

all the sleep of the previous season
diffused through the chest

making it rise and fall
under the heavy lid

to the sigh of stringed instruments
you only hear in your dreams.

THE CLOTHES-HANGER'S COLLARBONE

The clothes-hanger's head is a question mark
but he can shoulder your jacket
and his collarbone is firm enough
to take the weight of your skirts or trousers.

He may look frail
in the darkness of the wardrobe
but his wiry strength is impressive.

Nor should you underestimate
the apparently weak who stand in queues.
Think of all the work that each one does
in the darkness, at home, when no-one is looking.

Look at the conditions they survive in.
Touch their superhuman collarbones.

THE BOOK'S SPINE

Books are survivors.
They lay themselves open
to all kinds of dangers.

They stand in long rows
for anyone's inspection
and suffer the creatures;
grow foxed and dog-eared,
are nibbled by bookworms,
invaded by silverfish.

The voices inside them
are endless stories
of courage and failure
advance and retreat.

Their words march in columns
in slender files,
because authors die off but
the battle of the books is eternal.

No book is absolutely a closed book.
No book is utterly spineless.

A spineless book,
Not worth the price,
Too floppity-flop,
Too over-nice.

What I want's
A book with gut,
That springs wide open
And snaps shut.

THE WINDOW'S EYES

The window's eyes are glazed with constant staring.
Sometimes, the sky is all too bright,
the sun beyond bearing,
at other times the dark that comes at night
seems stuck there and it's getting very late
but you lie awake and wait
for all the stars to creep
across your half closed lids and sleep,

while the glass eyes of the houses all look out
reflecting on the streetlights, full of doubt.

THE BUTCHER'S CALVES

accompany him to work
and stand about waiting
as he goes about his business
growing tenser and darker
in the space above his socks.

They know what is afoot.
They've seen the leather of his shoes.

THE BOTTLE'S NECK

You may raise her by the neck
you may peer into her belly
and you can raise her hat
and watch her laughter
as she blows, bubbles and overflows

with the ridiculousness of everything
with relief and release
with high spirits
with air

THE CUP'S LIP

Whenever you try to take a sip
And raise the cup, it gives you lip.

It is a barefaced piece of cheek
Considering that cups can't speak,

Considering they make no sound
With just one lip, and that lip round.

A cup's a cup. You shouldn't stick it.
You're bigger and better. You can lick it.

THE ICE CREAM'S TONGUE

Just when you think you've got him licked
He whips round and licks you hollow,
That scoop you've left standing
On stilts like a tsunami wave
On the point of collapse
At the rim of the wafer
Licking your nose
And dribbling
Disgustingly
Like cat
Drool
Yuk

THE CAVE'S MOUTH

The cave gapes at the sea
As it has done for years,
Hardly able to believe
Everything it hears.

Strange echoes of its own
Gargles, sighs and groans
Are stored in its dark mouth
Like tiny bones.

Tiny bones of water
Trapped inside its throat,
The cave utters a sound,
Half cry, half musical note.

Cave language is like this:
it wells up from inside
but all it has to say
is swallowed by the tide.

THE LAKE'S BOTTOM

Don't even ask.
You don't want to know.
Whatever lives down there
Is unlikely to show.

The silent boat bobbing
Seems barely awake.
But something is throbbing
Deep in the lake.

In the Land of Giants

THREE MYSTERIES

1. THE LOST SOCK MYSTERY

They set out in pairs all over town
following in our footsteps
keeping their heads down
tucked safely away,
never going astray.

How was it then
that on their return to base
one of the pair got lost
in the very last place
you'd think it should disappear?
It was certainly most queer.

Where do socks go?
No one seems to know.
Nor MI5 nor the CIA
are yet prepared to say,

all hooded eyes
and enigmatic smiles.

One more case for the files.

2. THE MYSTERY OF THE ANT

The door was locked
so no one could get in
but somehow, over the table,
an ant came crawling
with a mischievous broad grin.

With a mischievous broad grin
the ant crawled on the table
as if to say it knew
of secret passages
that he could scramble through.

But if he could scramble through
the place was insecure and open to any bug.

No wonder he looked smug.

3. THE RAINBOW MYSTERY

One minute it was raining,
the sun had just peeked through,
and all things were as normal
when out of the grey and blue

this great big coloured arch
leapt into the sky
several miles wide, I guess,
and pretty near as high

and stood without permission,
over council land,
an unofficial structure
of the kind that we had banned.

No one had sought approval
or put in an application,
it was clearly a cowboy job
with ideas above its station.

And then it went clean missing
leaving nothing in its place
and the company that built it
is proving hard to trace.

IN THE LAND OF THE GIANTS

ROCK A BYE

Rock a bye baby
Sweet in your cot,

I am your mother
Like it or not.

Sometimes I like it,
Sometimes I hate it,

But baby you are far too young
For us to debate it.

For thou art a helpless babe, she sighed,
And kissed and rocked it gently as it cried.

BEWARE OF THE BEAR!

O parent behold your slumbering child
within the arms of the bear.
The animals round him are fearsome and wild
and threaten the babe in your care.

Wild asses, wild piglets, wild dolls and wild mice,
wild woomeroos stranger than dreams,
from realms of *Chaotic* and *Rough* and *Not Nice*,
from *Cities of Sorrows* and *Screams*.

O child, remember that tight little suit
you wore when you slept in your cot —
when you were still safe from the *Foul* and the *Brute?*
Well — once you get out you are not.

Caution's the word. The world can be awful.
You don't want to end up a grizzly bear's jawful.

IN THE LAND OF GIANTS

Once everything was big
and you were small,
but year after year your shadow
crept up the wall
and you grew tall.

Quite frightening really
to think of that small shadow disappearing,
to hear that small voice passing out of hearing.

That's the trouble with growing:
you'd like to know where you are going,
but there's no knowing.

AT GRAN'S

Come here my little one,
Come here wee man.
What has my baby done?
Tell your old gran.

The child viewed with deep alarm
The slow descent of her right arm.
His soul was hung about with crimes.
He could be troublesome at times.

FANCY DRESS

I'm dressed as a gnome though they think I'm a witch,
I've got a sore throat and my underarms itch,
I feel a bit feverish, I feel at a loss,
I'm lonely and tired and getting quite cross,
I hate stupid parties, I hate being a gnome,
I'm going to cry soon. I want to go home.

HENRY

Henry! she remarked,
It's months since you have had your ankles barked.

Henry! Henry! she hinted,
I do think you should have your eyeballs squinted.

Henry! Henry! Henry! she implored,
Do go out and get your fingers scored.

Henry! Henry! Henry! Henry! she desperately pleaded,
Haven't I always told you what you needed?

All all, all, all, all in vain.
Henry stood in disdain
And pondered heavy dark thoughts in his brain.

BRAVE

My mother said I never should
Play with the gypsies in the wood.

Beware of witches, toothless hags,
Torn skirts and bulging plastic bags

Beware of those whose lives look thin
Beware of liners from the bin

Beware of vast and empty spaces
Beware of scrubbed and empty faces.

I fix my clothes, I fix my stare.
I'm going out. Let them beware.

Let them beware and heed my call.
I'm going out to meet them all.

PIANIST

The pianist is full of grace,
His hands are bigger than his face.
Not the least part of his charms
Are fingers longer than his arms.
There is something almost comical
In a gift so anatomical.

SOULFUL

When you're feeling deeply doleful
When your soul is fully soulful
When you're choked and far from cheerful
When you need a tearful earful
When you're world-weary, heart-sick
Here's the man who'll do the trick.

He weeps and wails, he wears big rings,
He pours his heart out on the strings,
He makes the catgut throb,
He is a most mellifluous slob.

FLAUTIST

O melancholy sound, O Flute,
Your strands so cool, so convolute,
Unfolding gently as a petal,
Who would think you're made of metal?

I am tall and thin like you,
Your soundstream thrills me through and through,
My heart springs open like a brolly—
O flute, I too am melancholy.

PLUMBING SERVICE

My name is Fred Alcock.
I've come to fix your ballcock.

I've brought my spanners and my hammers,
My stuffers, scrapers, jammers,
My nippers and my rammers.

I see you've got some leaks.
This could take weeks.

EGG MAGIC

First the egg. You take and hold her SO.
Now do I see her? Do you see her? NO.
Egg, she gone, she disappear you bet!
That egg beat it so fast she omelette.

A little trick I learn and very queer,
But sure as eggs, good food she disappear

THE GREAT DRONGO

The Great Drongo in his cape and topper
Came an awful cropper
When, contrary to his usual habit,
He put bacon up his sleeve and fried the rabbit.

POET

See the poet, see the pipe
It's just as well to know the type:
His eyes are shifty, his beard shaggy,
His corduroys are always baggy,
His head is bald because the Muse
Has kissed away his hair,
His thoughts are misty and abstruse,
He fidgets in his chair.
By candlelight he sits and poses,
And, once in a blue moon, composes.

NO, LOVE

No, love, I'm just the cleaner
(They leave this place a mess!)
But if you've got complaints
Go see the manageress.

She's there in that small office.
Oh yes, I know she's in.
I swept her up an hour ago
And left her in the bin.

VISITOR

Hello, am I disturbing you?
I thought I'd just call by
To see if I could help in any way.
Oh, who am I?

I'm your neighbour, or almost.
Well, actually I live in Aberdeen
But I was passing Penzance and I thought,
Well, you know what I mean,

If I can help somebody as I pass along,
And I was passing, so . . .
But goodness me! Is that the time?
I think I'd better go.

MISS STRING

Swung on a swing,
A flower drooping in her hand.

Her neck was long,
Unlike this song.

AHEM

Ahem — as I was about to say,
In passing, so to speak,
I think it was but yesterday,
Or it might have been last week
The thought first struck me (if the phrase
Is not too bold — I mean
A thought *striking* a chap) to raise
An issue which has been
Preying on my mind since — well,

I hardly dare to think —
And I said to myself, *Oh what the hell,
Why blither on the brink,
Go out and start a sentence and
Just spring the thing on them,*
And then thought, *On the other hand* . . .
And so that's it. Ahem.

OLD COUPLES

Some lighter than leaves
Some wrinkled as water:
And each of them once
Was a son or a daughter.

Their fathers and mothers
Were children in turn;
Like water that dries,
Like leaves that must burn.

And here I stand waiting,
I'm still good as new,
My leaves are just grown

And I'm shiny with dew.

To be here at all
Is a reason for wonder
With so much to come
And so much gone under.

WHOOPSA

Whoopsa bobble, whoopsa bit
I don't have anywhere to sit,
Hi-de-hi, boop-boop-be-do,
If you don't look out I'll sit on you.

In the Land of Giants

MOONLIFE

MOON QUESTIONS

Is the Moon made of cheese?
Or has it a face?
The Moon is of rock
And its eyes are of space.

Does the Moon sing?
Does it make any sound?
No, there's only the silence
Of going round and round.

Can a cow jump
As high as the Moon?
No, if cows took to flight
They would land pretty soon.

Does the Moon waste away
And grow thin and then die?
No, it just looks that way
To an ignorant eye.

So is the Moon nothing
But folly and dreams?
And is there no magic?
So it seems, so it seems.

And yet I can feel her
Cool hands on my brow,
And see her reflection
In the eyes of the cow,

And I think I hear singing
Deep in my ear
That tells me she's rising
That tells me she's near.

So there are two worlds
Between which to choose
And what mind has to gain
The heart stands to lose?

Oh no, such a choice
There never has been.
The Moon is both rock
And a silver-faced queen.

Then what does the Moon do?
What does it say?
She draws up the tides and says
Come away, come away.

SPACE COMES OUT AT NIGHT

Space comes out at night
When stars look far away
And clouds stray
Across the moon
Like shadows on a silver tray

Space grows thick at night
When you're sure it's there
Not like in the daytime
When the sheer blank air
Is simply light
In flight

Space is when you know
That earth is not alone
That like other planets
It is a spinning stone

And you grow dizzy with the thought
Turning in your sleep
Which too is made of space
Dense and dark and deep.

And far beyond your dreams
Beyond their weightless mass,
Spin molecules and stars,
And fires and streams of gas

That wake to winter dark
In our spinning ark,
And you, small flickering spark,
You make your mark.

APPLE TREE

I saw a bride splendid in white garments
I saw a woman with one hundred children
The children plump and firm within her arms,
But some fell down or strangers took and ate them
Cut them, sliced them, bit them, baked them, boiled them —
Alas, alas, a widow frail and naked
Stood by my window in the heavy snow
Imagining, under the white snow. she was a bride again.
In time, she sighed, in time.

MOUSE DREAMING

Small as I am
I have such dreams
under the stairs,
the grey mouse screams.

In the dark hall
coats wave
empty sleeves,
enormous and grave.

But mouse just twitches
the end of his nose.
Well, dreams are for fulfilment,
I suppose.

GOLDFISH

Fire in water
A delicate flick of flame

All glow, gape and gill,
Now darting, now still

The soul
Of the bowl

But leisurely, leisurely,
Sunken treasurely,

ANIMAL LORE

The leopard laughs with lolling tongue
Hyenas hibernate when young
Giraffes all jeer at jokes and japes
Gorillas gobble up green grapes
Horses hee-haw when they're hoarse
Marmosets make notes in morse
Starlings stare and stare at stars
Buffalo binge on beer in bars
Dogs do good in dogged ways
Pigeons and pigs are fond of plays
Tigers tie grass in tangled knots
Hippopotami throw pots
Bears when bathing won't strip bare
Hares' haredressers hate their hair
Ants don't entertain their aunts
Platypuses plant few plants
Ewes use ewe-mail, bees just buzz,
Now you decide what the doe does.

THE WRECK OF THE HOPE

The Owl, the Flying Monkey and The Egg
All joined the Choir so they could learn to Beg.
One sang, one danced, the third stood on one Leg.

They sailed off in a leaky Ship of Fools.
Not finding Chairs they sat themselves on Stools,
Their feet immersed in darkly deepening Pools.

A piper in the Bow squeaked like a Shoe.
A fat man in the stern was all the Crew.
The sun had disappeared and the wind Blew.

The clouds were racing, bellowing like Deer,
The Flying Monkey jabbered full of fear.
The Egg cracked open grinning Ear to Ear.

With one great Hoot the Owl Gave up the Ghost
Just as they came in sight of the Last Coast,
But all were silent, none was left to Boast.

GEORGE SZIRTES

FROM THE HUNGARIAN

BIRD

Ottó Orbán

Alack, alack, alack
It's time to hit the sack.
The eyelid bird grows heavy, the sky is turning black.

The bird is singing, weep weep weep,
Time for Kate to go to sleep,
Look how mummy's eyes are closing
she herself is gently dozing.
Pussycat has long forgot
to purr inside her shoebox cot,
snoring somewhere in her head.
The little bird grows wings of lead.
Into the sack — I saw you yawn!
off with you now — Go fly till dawn.

THE SPRING

Ottó Orbán

Spring went off to school
grew into a stream
feet pattering over stones
as if in a dream

Having reached the fields
it widened into flood
grew thicker in the waist
green-brown with the mud

Once through with the world
it grew to adulthood.
In the grey Councils of the Sea
it sits, for good.

THE EARTH

Ottó Orbán

The Earth is round —
one great ball —
kid in the playground
shoots for goal —

ball flies high —
summer is nigh
ball descends —
the summer ends.

ANT

István Pákolitz

The ant is carrying a crumb
Assisted by his dad and mum,
They're hurrying because the wind
Is dragging great rainclouds behind.

Were I the wind I would waylay
The clouds and turn them all away
And scatter them across the sky
So that the ants could get home dry.

A POEM ABOUT TWO SEALS

Zoltán Zelk

The North Pole sweetshop tends to stay
Closed twenty-four hours a day,
Yet any time from nine till four
A sealboy and a sealgirl are
Sure to be waiting at the door.
What seals find enticing
Is cake with lots of icing!
And should you want cocoa made of snow —
The little polar corner shop
That never seems to open up
Is the only place to go.

WINTER TREES

Zoltán Zelk

Aren't you cold and won't you freeze,
With branches bare, you winter trees?
You've thrown away your summer shift,
Your autumn gold has come adrift.

Dearie me, you winter trees,
What strange behaviour, if you please!
In summer you could wear much less,
But come the winter — you undress!

STORKS

Zoltán Zelk

Stork so tall, long legged friend,
Where does the world begin and end?

You see the reeds there by the pond —
There's nothing of the world beyond.

Stork so tall with legs so thin.
Where then does the world begin?

Well stocked and fringed with fern and frond,
The pond is all. The world's the pond.

SNAIL

Ernö Szép

This, my child, is called a shell
The snail sleeps there, sound as a bell.

No use to call for Jack or Jim!
No clergyman has christened him,

His house has neither stair nor step
Nor hot nor cold water on tap,

No gas, no electricity,
A dwelling all simplicity,

And being small there's no fear that
A flying bomb should knock him flat.

It is indeed a house of bliss.
No peace to compare with this,

None to covet or to plot
To steal the treasures it has not.

Its virtues I will broadcast wide:
Its plain existence, lack of pride,

It will not disappoint nor fail
But serve as an exemplary tale.

THE BEAR'S DILEMMA

Sándor Weöres

Winter's going, here comes spring,
Grizzly bear sits pondering:
Back to sleep or time to wake?
What an awful choice to make!

To leave the cave? explore the wood?
There might be berries. Could be good.
And is the honey nice and sticky?
That is the question. Oh how tricky!

THREE SHORT VERSES ABOUT THE WIND

Sándor Weöres

1.

Wind whips up a gust,
Wind blows fit to bust,
Winter! thinks the bough,
What does wind want now?

2.

Wind will huff and wind will blow,
Wind goes mumbling to and fro.
However snug it is within
The wind succeeds in getting in.

3.

Roaring down the coastal shelf
The wind runs slap into itself,
Impossible to catch or check,
Its ankles high about its neck.

SLEIGHBELLS

Sándor Weöres

In deepest night you hear them ring,
The sleighbells go *ting ting a ling*,
Ting, ting a ling the sleighbells go
Faintly in the lap of snow.

Two enormous horses stop —
Eight hoofs pounding *clop clop clop*
Clop clop clop eight hoofs pounding
Down fields of silent deep resounding.

Forests of sound decomposing
Sleighbells splinter, *ding dong dozing*
Ding dong dozing sleighbells splinter
Against the far off rocks of winter.

DEEP IN THE WOOD THE VIOLETS DROWSE

Sándor Weöres

Deep in the wood
The violets drowse
Hidden beneath
Juniper boughs.
Why hide yourselves away,
Why not come out and play
In the light of day
Shy violets.

MY DOG ACE

György Végh

My dog Ace
won't wash his face.
My cat's called Butter
but this poem's not about her.
Is she any more keen
than Ace on being clean?
Tell us, Ace, since I suppose,
you'd know if anybody knows.

HAPPY NEW YEAR

Anon

Small as I am, I stand on the table
And shout as loud as I am able
So everyone should hear me call:
A Happy New Year to you all!